THE OPEN-FACED SANDWICH

12 Tasteful Tips to Effective Communication

By E. Earl Jenkins

Foreword by

Dr. Kenneth R. Hamilton

Scripture quotations are from the Holy Bible, New International Version®, NIV® Copyright © 1973, 1978, 1984, 2011 by Biblica, Inc.® Used by permission. All rights reserved worldwide.

Printed in the United States of America 2016 First Edition
10 9 8 7 6 5 4 3 2 1

Subject Index: Jenkins, Earl E
Title: The Open-Faced Sandwich: 12 Tasteful Tips to Effective Communication

1. Communication   2. Leadership 3. Business 4. Christian 5. Inspirational

Paperback ISBN: 978-0-9963858-0-0
Kindle ISBN: 978-0-9963858-1-7
Epub ISBN: 978-0-9963858-2-4

EE Jenkins Enterprises
9500 K Johnson Blvd. 3rd floor, Suite 2 Bordentown, NJ 08505
609-817-0055

Email: openfacedtips@gmail.com
theopenfacedsandwich.com

SANDWICH PRAISES...

"E. Earl Jenkins tackles the difficult and often misunderstood topic of communication in an engaging and memorable manner. Using the typical ingredients of a sandwich to dissect critical components of a conversation   or speech, Jenkins provides readers with unique insight and examples to deal with various personalities to get your point understood. Every ingredient of his open-faced sandwich has a specific purpose to bring an individual or audience to a common, tasteful understanding. An informative quick read for anyone who desires to be a better communicator."

Eric E. Jackson
Mayor, Trenton, New Jersey

"What blood is to the human body, communication is to every relationship. It is the transportation system that carries and conveys critical information and emotions to the right place. More often than not, every dysfunctional relationship is a symptomatic expression of a larger issue of ineffective communication. Just as the human body can't thrive without healthy blood, no relationship can thrive without healthy communication. In this insightful, concise, and highly practical work, *The Open-Faced Sandwich* Earl Jenkins provides us with 12 practical tips to revolutionize the way we communicate and consequently transform our relationships. His insight is unique, his approach is unconventional, and his information is accurate. You are 12 tips away from changing the way you communicate. After you read this book, people will really want to eat your words."

Dr. Dharius Daniels
Author of RePresent Jesus

"Learning to communicate effectively is a skill that everyone needs to master. *The Open-Faced Sandwich* provides a clever and easy to remember approach to making your point understood using key ingredients of a typical sandwich to communicate clearly. Whether you are speaking to your spouse, kids, your boss, co-workers, or a large audience, practicing the tasteful tips offered will strengthen your relationships, while building trust and respect in all of your personal interactions."

Kevin Johnson
CEO, KJohnson Enterprises

"Communication and success go hand-in-hand. Leaders in all arenas are constantly in need of improving their communication skills. Occasionally, someone provides unique insights that leaders must ponder and practice. In *The Open-Faced Sandwich: 12 Tasteful Tips to Effective Communication*, Earl Jenkins has creatively and clearly given insights that every leader can 'ponder' and should 'practice.' It is a must read."

Dr. Claude Thomas, President,
C3Global Dallas, Fort-Worth, Texas

To everyone who strives to be better communicators.

This bite is for you!

TABLE OF CONTENTS

FOREWORD

How often do we miscommunicate? Nothing in life is more important than knowing how to convey a message from one person to another. While advancements in technology have streamlined our ability to transfer information, it has also compromised our ability to be effective communicators. In this book, E. Earl Jenkins points us back in the direction of transferring meaning through purposeful communication. Not since *Who Moved My Cheese* has there been a more poignant application of good advice applicable to leaders across the spectrum. E. Earl Jenkins has managed to capture a clear, concise, analogy that everyone can relate to.

The Open-Faced Sandwich gives sound direction for improving communication and a handy reference guide for empowering others to walk into their full destiny. E. Earl Jenkins connects his experience as a pastor and church leader with his success as a businessman and entrepreneur. There is no better recipe for success than fusing these two callings.

Personally, I am inspired by this thought provoking, quick-read on building the perfect sandwich for success while guiding others along the road of self-actualization. He provides a mouthful of wisdom with this one. He's not preaching, but making biblical connections. If you can put together a simple open-faced sandwich, you can be a better communicator with the guidance in this book.

-Dr. Kenneth R. Hamilton

Taste This: *The name "sandwich" originated in Britain from John Montagu, the 4th Earl of Sandwich in the 18th Century. Montagu was an evil and corrupt aristocrat. During a 24-hour card binge at a local pub, he asked the waiter for roast beef placed between two slices of bread so he could pick up his snack with one hand and not get his cards greasy! Everyone around the table ordered the same thing and the "sandwich" was born. The sandwich continues to evolve and remains a favorite food around the world.*

The Tasty Open-Faced Communication Sandwich

Bread - Your personality
Meat - Your point
Cheese - Your timing
Lettuce - Your reasoning
Tomatoes - Your semantics
Mayo - Your transition
Mustard - Your complexity
Salt - Your flavor
Pepper - Your disposition

"It's not what you say that matters but the manner in which you say it..."

- William Carlos Williams

INTRODUCTION

"Good leaders must communicate vision clearly, creatively, and continually. However, the vision does not come alive until the leader models it."

- John C. Maxwell

Most people's general understanding of communication is that it involves a lot of talking. Yes, talking is just one aspect of this critical skill set. However, there is so much more connected in the process to get it right and communicate effectively. Whether you are speaking to your spouse, a colleague, one employee or a thousand, it is important that your message is understood in every encounter to avoid costly future misunderstandings.

Communication occurs when people exchange information or ideas. The key to any communication involves two or more people gathered for the same purpose.[EN 1] God Himself, the original communicator, was very intentional in communicating when He spoke the world into existence. Every word had meaning. His words created the same result when He established the church by bringing together a group of 19 nationalities in the Upper Room. The disconnect was that each ethnicity spoke a different language. Once His presence entered the room, everyone was with one accord. [EN 2] God strategized their means of communication to fulfill

His purpose to have more effective conversations and see positive results over time. People often ask me why I chose the title, *The Open-Faced Sandwich*. Although I do love healthy sandwiches, I'm not sure why God gave me a sandwich-themed communication strategy, but stay with me as I gather the bread, meat, lettuce, tomato and seasonings to help you become a more effective communicator. As a church leader and entrepreneur for nearly two decades, I believe this project was birthed out of my initial desire to help my staff and volunteers become better communicators.

In the church environment, I realized that I had been practicing the traditional "sandwich method" of communicating with direct reports. I provided positive feedback (a slice of bread), then offered a suggestion for improvement (a layer of meat), and followed it up with a positive comment (another slice of bread). In reality, I still found myself frustrated down the line because visible change never ensued. At that point, I realized that the "sandwich method" was ineffective. By dancing around my true issue with the person, I was sending a mixed message. I wasn't being totally honest with the true meat-my main point. In the long run, my ineffective communication left the person angry, confused, or resentful.

In hindsight, another reason I believe the "sandwich method" did not work was because the individual got wind of my routine and was not fully engaged in the conversation. He was already prepared to hear my message of his good work, then critique to do better, and wrap-up on a positive note. For example:

"You did a fantastic job with the teen program, Roger. Everyone thought it went well. Except you could have spent more time on working on the last routine. I also think you could have enlisted more audience and parent participation. Although it was a tough job, I thank you for taking on the challenge."

Sounds good, right? Maybe. The person is really unsure if I was genuinely satisfied with the program's outcome. My mixed message may have left him defensive or discouraged. Any future discussions could likely bring tension in the room.

As I continued to ponder my frustration and thoughts of a new and improved sandwich communication strategy, the old adage "honesty is the best policy" came to mind. Then the light bulb flickered on, and I envisioned an open-faced sandwich, uncovered, honest, with no hidden agenda in communicating. I thought, *Wow! This is an ideal method of communicating.* It has one less slice of bread, so you can focus on getting to the meat without worrying about adding the additional slice, which tends to send a mixed message anyway. People genuinely want to know the real deal in conversing without a lot of fluff. When you consider a shift in mindset to the open-faced method, you will see its benefits. Here's the previous conversation about the teen program's outcome using the open-faced method:

"Dillon, do you recall me asking you not to close out the program with that routine? I mentioned that it was over the heads of most of our teens and may anger some parents."

"You're right. It meant so much to me. I got a bit ahead of myself. I thought if you just saw the whole thing play out, you would be pleased."

"I figured as much, because I know that's how you think. I like that you are a proactive thinker. But please, next time let's make sure we are on the same page with these types of productions."

"No problem. I hear you."

"Okay good. Overall, I think you did a great job and everyone seemed to enjoy it. If I get any emails from unhappy parents I will forward them all to you to respond."

"Oh. Now, I really get it!"

We all know what a typical deli sandwich looks like. I'm not going to get to elaborate with specialized meats, imported cheeses, and twenty toppings because that would just make you hungry and distract from my message. You don't need to recite a one hundred page dissertation to tell an employee what you expect of him or her next quarter. All you need are a few key ingredients for your sandwich that will satisfy your desires and communicate your point. Don't worry about the layering, as you should only use what you need, since each item has a specific purpose. Therefore, if your point is made quickly, and the person is in agreement, then wrap up the conversation.

In order to make an open-faced sandwich, the first thing we need is a bottom slice of bread. I love whole wheat, so for my sandwich, that's my bread of choice. The *Bread* is both *your* approach and your personality that you bring to the communication. Whether you are familiar with your listener's personality or not, *your* approach will determine the outcome. Before I begin to add layers to my sandwich, I will spread mayo on my slice of bread to ensure my transitions, and the continuation of my message goes down smoothly.

The next important communication element in my sandwich is the deli meat. The *meat* is the driving point of what I want to say-without any additives or fillers. Don't waste too much time getting to the point because it is annoying and may cause your listener to tune out-especially if it's me! Then, I add lettuce, which is my reasoning: "Come let us reason together." [EN 3] The lettuce is my thought process in communicating my position. I may also add tomatoes, which has a variety of uses, but I want to make sure that you don't get too caught up in a semantic play on words, like you said "tomato," and I said "tomahto." Then, I sprinkle a little flavoring like salt and pepper to ensure candor and sincerity. Also, if needed, I can add a touch of mustard, so that difficult or complex subjects are broken down, highlighted, and understood.

My final element to my sandwich is a slice of cheese. The cheese allows me to go the extra mile by providing additional considerations to my timing and development to prepare a more tailored sandwich for my listener. Wait, don't dig in so fast! The sandwich needs to be cut in half. Cutting the sandwich represents the end of the conversation. Each party is departing the conversation with the same ingredients. Therefore, if you stick a toothpick on each side, both sides remain steady after departure. Whether a person feels good or bad about the conversation, at least she walks away with an understanding of why she felt that way.

My daily interactions with individuals are constant reminders of the importance of clear communication. Without it, we will continue running the gerbil wheel, engaging in the same stress-filled, unproductive conversations, over and over again. I have evolved and learned how to "finish" my open-faced sandwich, and have seen drastic improvements in my team's overall productiveness. Effective communication on a larger scale has become my next assignment that I humbly accept.

Whether you use a few of these sandwich ingredients, or all of them, this book will give you the essential tips towards open, useful, efficient, communication. You will be surprised by how much lighter you'll feel after eliminating stale, pointless, conversations that result in confusion, frustration, or missed opportunities. You will be equipped with two critical acronyms: T.A.S.T.E and B.R.E.A.D, to help you identify role in the communication, whether you are the speaker or listener.

It is my desire that you glean every morsel of your tasty open communication sandwich, so that you will build stronger business and personal relationships. Grab a napkin, wipe the crumbs from the corners of your mouth, as you satisfy your communication purposes with an effective open-faced sandwich.

Chapter 1
THE TASTE

Preparing Your Palate

"You have to get along with people, but you also have to recognize that the strength of a team is different people with different perspectives and different personalities."

- Steve Case

I know I'm not alone when I say eating is such a pleasurable experience. I always look forward to Sunday and holiday dinners with family and friends. There is something about the festiveness of the atmosphere and the aromas of old favorites and new dishes that make my mouth water. Taste is one of the five senses that is crucial to our health. Along with smell, it is a chemical sense that prepares our bodies for digesting food. If you lose your ability to taste, you will also lose your desire to eat, which can be detrimental to your overall health.

Understanding the aspects of taste is the first step to prepare you for effective conversations in your open-face sandwich model and by taking a look at how infants and toddlers explore the world gives you insight into this.

I have been blessed to have four grown children and three

grandsons. Now that I have officially earned the title "Pop," it's as if my grandchildren have awakened a keen sense of awareness that was buried inside me. I never actually gave much thought to how babies explored the world around them. The only real control infants have is in their lips and tongue to gum and mouth objects *before* they ever speak. The more infants "taste," the more they learn about shapes, textures, and their surroundings. When infants conduct their own mouth taste tests, they are testing the environment to make sure it's okay to continue exploring. So when my wife and I look after our grandsons, we pay extra attention to every item within their reach, because God only knows what they may have eaten by now!

With this "tasty" fact, we are similar to infants. The more comfortable we feel in our surroundings, the likelihood of a more positive conversation and outcome, even if it's a difficult subject. Think about a time when your wife called you into the bedroom to have a conversation. Did you pay attention to the surroundings when you stepped in? Was there soft music playing? Was the room tidy? Were candles lit? What did the look on her face reveal? What was her body language saying? If the ambiance in the room was dark, quiet, and untidy, chances are, you were in the dog house. Better yet, if her arms were folded, you may have wanted to stop back in for that talk a little later!

Similarly, when you step into a room to make a speech, check out the looks on the faces of the audience, their body language, and the sounds in the room. Does the majority of the audience look pensive, angry or happy? Are people talking or laughing? This will provide you with the tone you need to open your speech. Assessing the environment *before* you speak will give you a good idea of how to begin any conversation-it's your taste test.

When thinking of taste, consider the following:

T = Test
A = Assess
S = Stabilize
T = The
E = Environment

As you conduct an initial test of your environment, also assess the characteristics of the people in the room. Consider gender, roles and responsibilities, and audience interests when preparing your talk. Make sure you also take into account the positioning of the furniture, where you will sit or stand, and your posture. Finally, you should also maintain a reasonable distance from your listeners so that you don't overpower the room.

However, if you are in a one-on-one business meeting with a potential client, sit no more than three feet away from him or her since your main objective should be to build trust. Once you have addressed these issues and are comfortable that your environment is stabilized, then you are free to deliver your tasteful, satisfying, message!

Taste This: *Each of us has between 5,000 to 10,000 taste buds primarily on our tongue. Our taste buds only last 10-14 days and are constantly regenerating.*[EN 4] *Isn't it refreshing to know that you can also change and improve your communication style as well?*

YOUR TASTE BUDS

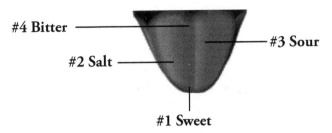

#4 Bitter

#3 Sour

#2 Salt

#1 Sweet

Which Tasty Communicator Are You?

There are four basic tastes: sour, sweet, salty, and bitter. Until now, I never realized how all of these tasty words are commonly used to describe a person's communication style or personality. I actually don't mind sour, the acid-like tastes of lemon and vinegar. However, sour communication is negative, and is usually the end of personal or business relationships. When an establishment or people leave a "sour" taste in your mouth, you may want to reevaluate the relationship.

Let's take a look at these different kinds of people:

SOUR

Jeff: Round up the crew so we can all go to that really nice seafood restaurant on 8th Street this weekend.
Leslie: Oh yes, that place was great. But please, whatever you do, don't invite Mike this time.
Jeff: Why not? I thought everyone liked Mike.
Leslie: To be honest, Jeff, Mike is your friend, and no one likes him.
Jeff: Why?
Leslie: Well, Mike left a bad taste in everyone's mouth because he never pays his fair share of the bill!

In this example, Mike the "free-loader" left a sour taste the few times he went out with the group and it became difficult to change this impression.

SWEET

Most people like sweets. I actually never had a sweet-tooth, but I will overindulge in my mom's peach cobbler. Chocolate is a powerful mood- enhancer, and makes us feel good. When someone has a "sweet" disposition or communication style, she will more likely win people over. Regardless of her message, she will be well-received. Sweet is also used to describe all things pleasurable and good. [EN 5]

Sweet and sour are commonly thought of as opposites. Many cultures have food or sauce combinations to satisfy these polar opposite pallets. Lately, I've noticed more snack products offering a "sweet and salty" variety. Our taste buds are signaling our brain, wanting the sweetest and saltiest foods at the same time. Of course, we all need small doses of salt and sugar in our diet, however, too much of either is unhealthy, and can be dangerous.

SALTY

If someone has ever called you *salty*, just know that it is not a compliment! You probably came across as highly irritated, angry, or downright ugly. Being described as salty will definitely lead to the end of the conversation, or the relationship as a whole. My wife and I recently walked into a local restaurant for the first time. We both smiled and greeted the hostess.

Me: Table for two, please.
Hostess: You do know there is await!
Me: Actually, no I didn't. We're the only people standing

here!

Hostess: Like I said, it's a wait! We're changing shifts and setting up for dinner. Maybe you should try someplace else!

Me: We certainly will.

Needless to say, I turned toward the exit and the manager pleaded with me and my wife to stay. He told us that the hostess was having a bad day after an encounter with a difficult customer during lunch. I know we all have our days, but if you work in a customer service capacity, you must practice controlling your emotions so that you can quickly turn it back "on" for the next customer. Saltiness has consequences. If you don't change your attitude, you'll likely end up on the unemployment line.

BITTER

Whenever I think of a "bitter" taste, I think of someone out for revenge. If a person has been offended or hurt in the past, they may harbor a grudge that leads to bitterness. Communicating with a bitter person is difficult, as he will tend to zone out on whatever you are saying, because he can't get past what happened between the two of you previously. A bitter person comes across as unreasonable, as his mindset is narrowly focused. From a taste perspective, coffee, citrus peels, and beer are all bitter, yet people's taste buds find them enjoyable. With patience and practice, you can also find a bitter person pleasant to talk to.

Preparation is the key. Everyone is unique and has his or her own tastes. Know going in what type of *tasty* personality you are dealing with, and build your sandwich accordingly.

Sweet Peppers:

Take time to gather information about the person you will be communicating with if it is your first encounter. The more research and insight you have on the person, the more likely you will have a favorable outcome. Healthy relationships are built on open and honest communication.

YOUR TASTEFUL APPROACH

You can satisfy your communication appetite by being open and honest. Studies have shown that people trust leaders who they believe are transparent. Transparency also tells the listener you have mutual respect for him or her. Openness allows a dialogue exchange that gathers input from others. If you are the boss, this lessens the fear or intimidation employees may have when speaking with you. If you are the head of your household, your spouse and children will be comfortable providing input to family decisions. What if you are communicating with colleagues? Try being open to eliminate jealousy, gossiping and backstabbing for upcoming positions.

> *Margie:* Lisa, I want you to know that I just put my hat in the ring for the senior manager position. I overheard people talking yesterday and they said you applied as well. At the end of the day I think we'd both be great at it.
> *Lisa:* I agree. When I saw it, you were the first person that came to mind.
> Then I told my husband about it and he said I should go for it to show my initiative and commitment to the company.
> *Margie extended her hand to Lisa and they shook.*

> **Lisa:** Regardless of the outcome, I know we can make it work.

As you can see from this colleague-to-colleague conversation, there are several benefits to being open. First, it eliminates any whispers as to whether you are seeking advancement, and you can both be at ease and allow for a more positive conversation. Second, your colleague will feel like you value him or her by being proactive and letting him know your position. I can't tell you how many people put their foot in their mouth at work by back-biting each other for a position, without realizing that everything said will be held against them! The colleague whom you have complained and gossiped about yesterday, may be your new boss today! I wholeheartedly believe that God's plans for you are just that-specifically for you. There is no need to be jealous, cross, or verbally attack someone when you are seeking a blessing. Instead of treating a colleague like your worst enemy, take her out to lunch!

There can only be one you. Therefore, no one can beat you at being you. Focus on being your best everyday. If you truly believe that you're the best at what you do, there is no need to try to make yourself appear bigger or better than the next guy. Did you ever notice how Burger King always went after McDonald's with negative advertising? McDonald's refrained from putting down other companies in their advertising campaigns. Although their rankings may have slipped recently, McDonald's has held the number one spot in the fast-food industry for several years. It's tough being on top because the competition is always salivating for every opportunity to grab a bite of your market share, which can be stressful as a leader. Yet using your knowledge and skills to "eat" the competition and not your employees may be the deciding factor in fortune or failure.

EAT UP!

Before engaging in an important communication, consider the taste acronym:

T= Test, **A**=Access, **S**=Stabilize, **T**=The, **E**=Environment.

Your Sides
Senior Manager to Employee

Ask probing questions to set the tone to get the employee talking first.

Admit when you don't know something.

Don't send mixed messages.

Be vulnerable to develop trust.

Relationships

Don't postpone important conversations, however make sure environment is conducive for hearing each other out.

State your needs upfront in a kind tone.

Listen before you speak.

Potential Client

Do your homework so you will focus on client's needs.

Discuss other client success stories.

Demonstrate how you can exceed their expectations.

Chapter 2
The Bread

Your Personality

"...If you're a leader and you're the smartest guy in the world-in the room, you've got real problems."

- Jack Welch

Everyone is unique and has his or her own leadership style. In my open- faced sandwich model, the *Bread* is your personality and your approach as the communicator. As a leader, your authority is only a position that enables you to have the power of influence over those under you. Your influence is a direct reflection of your personality that people tend to follow or reject. I have defined leaders' personalities in a bread theme to demonstrate the effect your personality has on the outcome of your discussions. Which type of leader are you?

Taste This: *Bread is a cross-cultural staple. Many ethnicities, races, countries and religions use bread in ceremonies and view it as peace offering.* [EN 6]

Enriched Leaders can strip their staff of key ingredients not allowing them to successfully do their job.

Whole Wheat Leaders tend to be open and engaging with their staff and show value for their gifts and talents by empowering them to make decisions.

Multigrain Leaders have healthy qualities, yet they may have delegation challenges and often try to do everything themselves.

Flatbread Leaders often exhibit a narrow focus because they only see one way of doing things, which hinders creativity and growth.

Rye Leaders are calm under pressure and remain "standing" under extreme challenges.

Hoagie Leaders are extremely likable and create fun environments. They are everyone's friend, however, these types of leaders have difficulty making tough decisions for fear of being disliked.

ENRICHED LEADERS

Enriched leaders are those who lead with a strong-arm and pull out qualities from their employees only for the leader's benefit. Such leaders typically dictate orders and have no shame in stripping employees of their ideas and character. Most enriched leaders use their people as a platform to push their selfish, personal agendas. I've also seen many enriched leaders on a quest to hire clones of themselves. They become blind to the fact that the new "leader-double" will never become great, because he is being controlled without utilizing any of his unique qualities.

WHOLE WHEAT LEADERS

Whole wheat leaders focus on getting their point across in a clear, concise and honest manner. These types of leaders are not fixated on a scholarly vocabulary that sounds good. Instead, they humble themselves and speak on the level of their audience. Whole wheat leadership is not passive, but rather aggressive in developing employees with good intentions toward the common goal of the company.

In order to be an effective whole wheat leader, you should have a personal relationship with your executive team, one built on trust and respect.

Whole wheat leaders garner support from their employees because the majority of employees truly believe the leader personally cares for them. Such a strong belief equates to committed employees working hard to provide the best product or service to customers. One of my favorite TV shows is *Undercover Boss*. This show depicts bosses disguised as average employees working side-by-side with their peers. Being in the trenches gives the boss a glimpse of the employee's challenges and attitudes toward their job. In the end, it is usually the boss who gets a rude awakening, and becomes more compassionate toward his staff. In nearly every show, the boss becomes privy to the personal trials someone is enduring, as she works tirelessly to make the company a success. Many of the bosses in *Undercover Boss* have transformed into whole wheat leaders from their experiences.

MULTIGRAIN LEADERS

Multigrain leaders have all the right nutrients and ingredients to foster a healthy work environment. They are multi-talented, optimistic, "people- lovers," and can charm the best of us. However, to their detriment, multigrain leaders attempt to "be all" and "do all" in their organization. These types of leaders lack delegation abilities because of their tendency to be perfectionists. Additionally, the desire to be "perfect" may come across as a lack of trust in their staff. Multigrain leaders have the best intentions, but fail to accomplish projects as there will never be enough time in a day to walk in their leadership role and perform the job of five staff members. Multigrain leaders will burn- out quickly.

As a leader, your goal is to hire the right people to perform their jobs. Allow your employees to grow and demonstrate that they are qualified to do what you pay them for. Your spouse will thank you.

FLATBREAD LEADERS

Most flatbread leaders have been in their role and industry for several years. In their minds, they have seen it all. Flatbread leaders generally see things as black or white. Gray is outside of their mental or visual capacity. Flatbread leaders are "flat," satisfied with the status quo. They tend to be apprehensive about change, and are okay with just surviving.

Great leaders create a long-term vision that results in growth and innovation. If you are adverse to fresh ideas, inflexible, and stuck in the past, failure is inevitable.

RYE LEADERS

The strong flavor of rye bread is a similar characteristic to a rye leader. Rye bread does not rise, so a rye leader is cool and calm under extreme pressure. There is never a sense of panic, as rye leaders are in tune with their emotions. Rye leaders are able to make everyone feel safe after tragedy strikes. Rye leaders accept responsibility and are accountable for their actions when a decision did not go as planned.

HOAGIE/HERO LEADERS

Hoagie leaders are all-around nice guys, and make everyone feel as if they're a close friend. The basic problem with this type of relationship is that friends should be equal. If you are the boss, then equality diminishes. As a hoagie leader, how can you provide critical feedback to your friend? Can you fire her? As friends, you get to know intimate details about a person, and that can be a distraction or hindrance to work. Always keep in mind that the primary purpose of the relationship is for the worker to get job done.

I believe Spiritual leaders fall into the hoagie category because they have a heart to help everyone. Oftentimes, spiritual leaders are taken advantage of in the business world because others mistake their kindness for weakness. Spiritual leaders must demonstrate their business acumen when necessary.

As you can see, there are several types of bread-based leaders that contain various personalities. It is important to find that balance in your leadership personality as you strive to be an effective communicator-more like a whole wheat leader.

Whole wheat leaders bring out the best in their people and are successful in effectively communicating on a daily basis. Changing your leadership style may be difficult at first, but with concentrated efforts to change and practice, growth and success are inevitable. Your goal is to strive for 100 percent of tasty effective communications from here on out. Stay hungry my friend!

YOUR PERSONALITY AND APPROACH

As a leader, your approach to the communication is critical. However, equally important is your personality. Your bread personality will make all the difference in either your success or failure in getting your message understood.

ENRICHED LEADERSHIP

I grew up eating "enriched" and "fortified" white bread. Even though both of these types of bread sounded like they were healthy and of a better quality than other bread, they were not.

Enriched bread is actually stripped of its original nature by the manufacturer who adds bleach and chemicals to make it *taste* good. I must admit, as a child, white bread was delicious! As I got older, I realized how bad it was for me. White bread lacks nutrients and spikes your blood sugar level, which causes health problems. Eating white bread and other "fortified" carbohydrates ultimately leads to weight gain.

The same can be said about enriched leaders. Take this example of Edward, a new employee and Stan, his boss.

ENRICHED LEADER PICKLE

Edward was excited to start his new job at one of the top strategic marketing firms in Philadelphia. He'd been at the top of his game, the envy of his colleagues at his previous firm, and now he was anxious to begin this new challenge.

He'd made it through the round-robin interviews for two months and after being hired, was assigned to a project, which he was more than capable of handling. Edward embarked on his task of developing a ground-breaking strategy for the client and after several months, was prepared to make his presentation.

He put in the time, he put in the effort and on the day of his presentation, he was more than ready. To Edward, his boss, Stan appeared genuinely eager to have him on board, however the rest of the staff knew otherwise.

On the day of the presentation, Edward stood in front of the team, and began his presentation. He was more than halfway through when Stan stood and motioned for Edward to sit down.

His boss was now front and center using Edward's Power-Point presentation. It was confusing to Edward, but he continued talking from his seat.

Edward: So as you can see, I have created a solution that is unprecedented in this type of setting.
Colleague: I must say Ed, you're right. I have never seen anything quite as turnkey as this.
Stan: Actually, I created a similar plan two years ago. I was waiting for the right time to expose it. But since you brought it up, we can now entertain it.
Edward: Is there anything I can add to make this better?
Stan: No, no. We will work with what you have here. You can just sit back. I'll take over from here.

Right before everyone's eyes, his boss stole the show and presented Edward's work to the team as if it were his own. Every time Edward chimed in to emphasize a point, Stan downgraded his input.

By the end of the meeting, Edward felt frustrated and incompetent. He couldn't figure out why his boss had behaved that way. The next day, Edward was talking with his colleagues about the presentation fiasco. Linda, shared her personal views on their boss.

Linda: Ed, I've been around here for a while, and I have seen Stan at his best and his worst. Stan is a brilliant man, however, he is very insecure and feels threatened if someone comes across as more brilliant than him. He is afraid that clients will not see his value and eventually steal one of us away.
Edward: But that doesn't make sense. He hired us because we are qualified. We love what we do. If he treats us fairly, why would we want to leave?

Linda: I can't answer that. But I can let you in on a little secret.

Edward: What's that?

Linda: The rest of the staff and I have stopped working so hard on   these types of projects because Stan is just going to take full credit for them anyway. Even if he only adds one sentence, rest assured, he will come back to you and tell you that if it wasn't for his input, the client would have walked away.

Insecurity is a common thread amongst enriched leaders. Such insecurity often leads to a brazen embarrassment of people whom that leader deems more intelligent or popular than him. This is what I call the enriched leader pickle - a leader with a personality problem that has no easy answer because it stems   from a long-term character flaw. Enriched leaders stifle their organizations when they are afraid to let go of the reins; enriched leaders are afraid to allow others to use their talents.

To the surprise of the staff, this same leader complained about the growth of the organization, while never owning up to the fact that he had been the major hindrance to growth all along. Devaluing and undermining staff efforts to provide client solutions, this leader ultimately discouraged Edward and his peers from producing their best work.

After four months of the constant belittlement, Edward started having feelings of resentment toward his boss. He withdrew from the team and did not offer his input on future projects. He did only exactly what was asked of him, and not long after that, began sending out his resume.

Through my experiences, I have found that you can "enrich" someone while also allowing them to shine in the qualities you hired him or her for. It's not difficult to take a step back and allow an employee to operate and grow independent of your influence. Once you do this, you will see creativity and other desirable assets come forth in that employee. Just think about it, what was the point of hiring him or her in the first place? Were you really seeking a mini-you?

Many enriched leaders unintentionally strip employees of their strengths and good qualities. At one time, Apostle Paul was an enriched leader. He was focused on protecting the faith at the expense of slaughtering Christians who had a different perspective of God EN 7. Paul's erroneous thinking limited the goal of Christianity to his personal viewpoint and because of that, he did everything in his power to make sure that the faith did not grow.

However, once Paul recognized Jesus' position, Paul changed his perspective of Christianity and admonished others to do the same. Paul received an increased portion of God's power, which allowed him to effectively communicate with others and treat them with love and respect.

Most enriched leaders hinder an organization's progress. They are so focused on their leadership titles, that the titles literally end up going to their heads. They believe that others are beneath them, which stirs up unnecessary internal tension. Due to these negative personality traits, employees of enriched leaders feel less valuable and end up resenting the leader and the organization. As a result, these employees retreat and never give their best, which in the end hurts the organization. From a retention perspective, these unmotivated and unappreciated employees end up leaving the organization.

Enriched leaders must recognize these weaknesses and get out of their own way. These leaders should embrace a new way of approaching relationships by adding portions of reasoning to their thought processes. What can an enriched leader do to change? The first thing you have to do is see it; sometimes that is difficult for an enriched leader to see himself that way. However, all an enriched leader has to do is consider his or her retention rate, which should give him a clue.

There are steps that you can take to build morale and retain employees. For starters, throw away the sour pickle, which is distracting you from seeing your negative behavior toward others. Pickles are extras; things that you tend to focus on that are not part of the larger problem. Come clean with yourself. There is hope for reincarnation without added chemicals or bleaches. There is hope to get you on a path to a healthier you, which will lead to better interactions with others.

Whether you are leading a billion dollar company, a small business, or your household, if you want to be a great leader in your arena, it requires hard work, dedication, and a strong commitment to your core team. You must change your perspective and see the value in all people—not as possessive objects or mere employees. As you interact with a new mindset of embracing what others bring to the table, you should feel more at ease that their contributions can only enhance your life and your organization. Your goal is to motivate and empower everyone you are charged to lead, so that they can operate at peak performance, which will actually make you look like a genius for hiring them!

WHOLE WHEAT LEADERSHIP

Leaders must be confident, charismatic, and compassionate in order for others to follow and that's what whole wheat leadership is all about. The greatest example of healthy, whole wheat leadership is Jesus. In fact, scripture defines Him as "the bread of life." [EN8]

One of the main reasons Jesus had a great following was because of his method of communication. Jesus spoke in parables, a simple story to illustrate a moral lesson. Whole wheat leaders are effective communicators without diminishing the key qualities of their employees. Peter, James, John, and Matthew, ultimately became great authors of the New Testament church, all because of the whole wheat leadership of Jesus. "Let this mind be in you that was also in Christ Jesus." [EN 9]

Most of us would have discounted Peter from the door. Despite Peter's faults, Jesus knew what he brought to the table. Think about that because Jesus was able to eliminate anyone who was detrimental to His cause.

Even with Judas, Jesus knew of Judas' plot to betray Him, yet, Jesus' method of communication was sensitive and concise. Remember, Jesus never terminated Judas-Judas terminated himself. [EN 10]

100% Team Effort

As a business leader and pastor, I know that people are watching my every move and listening to everything I say-especially what I say from the pulpit. The revelation that was given to me of enriched and whole wheat leadership had me thinking about my own leadership style and whether I could improve the quality of my words. After careful analysis, I realized that I had spent my life striving to be a whole wheat leader.

Even when I worked in corporate America, I carried a very humble personality, which allowed me to consider how the person I was communicating with would receive my message. As a result of that trait, people often came to me and shared their private issues. I had an ability to communicate what people needed to hear, good or bad. No matter what the message was, people were able to leave my presence without feeling discouraged.

Looking back, this is a skill I've had all my life. I've been able to provide constructive criticism to others in the most compassionate, candid manner I know, never stripping someone of their self-worth. I was always a whole wheat leader without ever realizing it. However, even as a whole wheat leader, I've had some challenges. I must admit that for many years, I expected too much from my staff and volunteers. I often felt that they were not as committed to a particular project as I was.

Then it hit me one day that it is impossible for a person to give you 100 percent of himself. We all have so many daily responsibilities and distractions that we cannot commit 100 percent to anything. For example, if you are married with children, your spouse and kids may take 30 percent of your efforts and thought process on any given day, whether they are in your presence or not. Additionally, if you have other responsibilities like caring for a parent, financial stress, or a second job, then those responsibilities or situations may take 20 percent from you.

After looking at it this way, the light bulb came on. I realized that it was never a commitment issue; people were just giving me what they had left. That was when I began to see that a person might only have 50 percent to give toward my goal. Once I realized that, I decided that what I needed was not one person committed to 100 percent; I needed a dedicated team to get the task done. If everyone on the team gave 100 percent of what was left of them, then the project would be 100 percent completed.

I began to focus on the "assembly line" where each person did his part to contribute to the success of the whole. However, just because you may be working with an assembly line, doesn't make communication any less important.

If your team is in fact an assembly line process, each person plays a vital role in communicating with one another, as well as with potential customers. Each and every person on the assembly line must have effective communication skills, with no room for miscommunication. This is important for everyone to understand because if one person in the line is having a bad day and does not provide the correct ingredients in communicating, that person could cause problems and havoc for the whole team.

If your sandwich is built by you or on an assembly line, the key factor to success is your commitment to the task at hand. The primary objective is to create an open-faced sandwich of communication with all of the necessary ingredients to make your point understood. As the leader, you must understand that communication is not just about you speaking. It is as much about you listening and respecting the other person's response and opinion. Only then can you move forward in a positive manner.

Remember, as the initiator of the discussion, you are responsible for each layer of communication. If the sandwich requires group input, then ensure that each person in the group understands his responsibility of adding meat, lettuce, tomatoes, mayo, or other seasonings for a productive outcome.

Sweet Peppers:

As a whole wheat leader, keep a holistic view of not just your product or service, but also the people who make it happen.

THE WHOLE WHEAT ADVANTAGE

Today, the media and other forms of advertising constantly feed us the benefits of eating whole wheat and whole grain bread. I should mention that whole wheat bread with whole grains or whole oats are the healthiest options because they are loaded with vitamins and minerals. The same is true with communication; a whole wheat leader never loses his ability to communicate because his natural tendency is to speak from the heart and be a blessing to others.

Again, being a compassionate leader will keep you sensitive to the needs of your employees. It's hard to see the picture while you are in the frame. Jesus got down in the trenches not to stay there, but to relate to those who supported and followed Him. "For we have not a high priest which cannot be touched with the feeling of our infirmities, but was in all points tempted like as we are yet without sin." EN 11

Sweet Peppers:

As a leader, I challenge you to lead with influence as if you were following yourself. If you take on this mindset, you are governing your leadership with a level of sensitivity toward your staff, who are the key people you ultimately need to complete your unified goal.

EAT UP!

Manager to Employee

Don't wear your title as a badge of superiority. Employees will trust you and be more open interacting with you if you ditch the "I'm the boss" persona.

Don't be afraid to share your background if you struggled throughout life to get where you are now.

Spouse

Show empathy when communicating with your spouse. If the conversation is difficult, he or she will need to feel that you understand.

In challenging times, provide words of comfort or examples previous challenges that you both overcame or stories of others who persevered under similar circumstances.

A Few Crumbs...

I cannot stress the relevance of choosing the right "bread" approach to making your sandwich. Bread is a key ingredient for livelihood, and is often used in slang to mean money, which we all know is important, and has its place. Think about a few common sayings that relate to bread as you prepare to deliver your sandwich communication. You will be surprised to see how these phrases capture the essence of points you intend to make, especially if you ***know what side your bread is buttered on!***

•When you sit down to have the discussion, visualize yourself ***breaking bread*** with your associates. This will make you more relaxed and a bit vulnerable which may be necessary in the conversation.

•Generally, people need to feel that they can trust your actions and words. So consider ***casting your bread*** upon the waters to make them feel comfortable, and that your actions are genuine and generous. Let them see that you are not seeking to personally benefit from the communication. Never make your listener feel like you are ***taking the bread out of his mouth.***

Chapter 3
THE MEAT

Your Point

"The most valuable of all talent is that of never using two words when one will do."

- Thomas Jefferson

Regardless of the situation, both parties must have a clear understanding of the real issue-the meat of the conversation. The meat represents the point you are trying to make in the communication, and it is the next layer of your open-faced sandwich. It is your sole purpose for speaking in the first place.

I know that many of you traditionally place the extras at this layer, like vegetables and other sides, but if you can get to the point right away, then by all means do so. If you find yourself rambling, and not saying what you really want to say, stop and go straight to the point. I call this the toothpick approach. I suggest using this approach when you are in a one-on-one conversation. Forget about your prepared conversation. Stick a toothpick in their words of agreement, and end the conversation by saying, "Wow, that sounds good. I'm glad you see it that way. Let's talk again soon.

So often we are guilty of adding a lot of fluff when communicating in order to appear well-versed in a particular subject matter. Or sometimes, we add a lot of words to delay getting to the point because we want to spare someone of an unpleasant truth. All of those extra words can quickly turn your listener off. A person knows when you are buying time or stalling. Be cognizant of this; you don't want to give too much bread and not enough meat.

I was talking to my mother recently about why she no longer patronized the sandwich franchise near our home.

> **Mom:** I drove ten miles out of my way to go to the other sandwich shop across town.
> **Me:** Why did you do that? I thought you liked the one down the road.
> **Mom:** Well I used to, but I noticed the last two times they gave me very little meat and too much bread!
> **Me:** Why didn't you tell them you weren't satisfied?
> **Mom:** There was no need. It's worth going a little out of my way because the other shop gives the right amount of meat!

Today, most of us are operating with a full plate of responsibilities and would rather spend our money and time elsewhere if we aren't getting enough meat to keep us satisfied. It doesn't matter what type of meat or vegetable you choose as the main substance of your communication sandwich, just know that it is the most important part.

If the meat is a touchy or uncomfortable subject for an individual or group, practice opening lines to put them at ease.

For a group, you may want to say something like, "I know you are all unsure of what's happening right now, but take comfort in knowing that at the end of the day, we will all be better off.

If you're dealing with an individual, it may be useful to indirectly test the environment by making a comment to the person about the uncomfortable message. This is just to see how they react before engaging deeper into the conversation. Based on their reaction, you will know the right ingredients to use to build your open-faced sandwich.

> **Taste This:** *Adults today have a sustained attention span of five minutes. However, you must capture a person's attention in the first 8.25 seconds, which is one second less than the attention span of a goldfish!* EN 11 *Be engaging and make your point quickly or you've wasted your time.*

Early in my career, one of the biggest mistakes I made in communicating with my staff was over emphasizing a point that prolonged the conversation. Whenever I did this, by the end of my talk, most people lost the essence and flavor of what I was originally trying to say. I have learned over time that a conversation to discuss an aspect of change, negative employee behavior, or other organizational challenges, should take no longer than 20 minutes! With psychologists disagreeing over short- term and long-term attention span, try to speak in no longer than 20 minute intervals. Allow time for breaks, Q&A, and group assignments, so attendees can refocus their attention. Here is a key point: If you don't have a clear and concise message, then don't have a conversation; there's no need for you to say anything. Wait until you have something of substance to relay, or you will lose credibility.

Here is another point for you to remember: if you have worked on something for a long time, it may be difficult to convey it clearly to others. Doing the work and explaining it requires two different techniques. Once you have created and lived with something, it becomes a part of you. That makes it difficult to step outside of that knowledge sphere. Having a definite message with information that will help move the situation or relationship forward, is one of the keys to being an effective leader and communicator.

Here are a few scenarios about how to (or not to) get to the meat of the conversation:

Years ago, I was charged with releasing an employee in corporate America that no one in the division had the guts to fire. Of course, I did not want to be the bad guy either. But through process of elimination, the task fell on my plate. My task: I had to fire a single mother with two children.

Lindsey was by far, one of the greatest workers I had ever encountered. She was a quick learner, and truly did her job better than anyone else. However, her division was being shut down.

As tough as it was, I immediately got to the meat of the conversation and told her that the company was downsizing. I got to the point-that good people like herself had to be let go. Yet, at the same time I wanted it to be clear that the downsizing was temporary, and that we might call her back in the future. My primary focus was to ensure that she did not leave the company as a disgruntled ex-employee.

I then added mayo (something I will talk about later) to smooth over the rest of the conversation, as I told her how wonderful she was as an employee and a team member. I complimented her on the good job she'd done raising her children. I wanted to make sure I empowered her as a person, and communicated to her that her efforts had helped us grow into the corporation we were today.

In addition, I wanted to alleviate any sense of fear that she had about finding another job, because based on what I saw, she was a true warrior. Not only was she ambitious, she was resilient and could weather this temporary storm.

After our conversation, she smiled, stood up, shook my hand and said, "I have never been fired so nicely."

A few months later, we called to hire her back. But we were too late.

She was already working for another company. To my surprise, I received a phone call from her boss who invited me out to lunch. He told me how impressed he was with her and thanked me for training such a wonderful worker.

***

I recall waiting outside the office of a consultant, and I overheard a conversation between her and another business owner. As the meeting was nearing the end, she said, "Listen, don't sandwich me in."

I smiled because she was a sharp businesswoman, and I'd heard her say those words in the past. In my eyes, her comment had a two-fold meaning: First, she was letting the guy know that she did not want him to bluff her by just saying things that she wanted to hear. Second, she was saying that she did not want to feel locked into one thought process when he really meant something else.

This is similar to not providing enough meat on purpose-like a salesman's pitch.

Another scenario where getting to the meat of your discussion is critical happens in those instances when you have to be assertive in making your point understood. You may find yourself saddled with someone else's method to make a situation happen a certain way on your behalf.

However during the conversation, you realize that it is up to you to take charge. Take the lead by making a quick and decisive hard line in the conversation so that you don't get sandwiched into something you had no intention being involved with. Make your point.

These are just three examples of how crucial it is to not only make your point, but to make your point quickly. Get to the meat of your conversation because a lot of people won't like all the extras-no cheese, lettuce, tomato, mayo or anything else. Many people just want it plain. When you leave out all the extras, it may turn the conversation around in your flavor, I mean favor!

Sweet Peppers:

With so many outside distractions, and a listener's limited attention span, be concise and leave out irrelevant information. Provide visual bullets of your main points or speak in terms "first, second, last," so at least the person walks away with a few key points and items to focus on. Check in to confirm your listener's understanding and ask if there are any questions.

EAT UP!

With only a limited time for your message to be received, be clear about your priorities, be current, and most of all be complete, especially when launching a new product offering.

Large Audience

🍴 Create excitement prior to launch
🍴 Speak in "headlines" to capture attention
🍴 Provide visuals of current product & new product

Solicit questions and feedback

"You don't need a pack of wild horses to learn how to make a sandwich."

- Dr. Phil McGraw

A Few Crumbs...

When people think of meat, they tend to think of it in terms of flesh from an animal. Yet for our purposes, think of the meat as the best layer or best part of the communication. Try to envision the meat as the "juicy" chunk of a piece of fruit or the plentiful part of a nut. Again, make it good and to the point as it will be the listener's main takeaway

Chapter 4
THE CHEESE

Your Timing & Development

"Think as wise men do, but speak as the common people do."

- Aristotle

Of course, all open-faced sandwiches do not have melted cheese on top, but for our sandwich it does. What's so great about cheese? The cheese in your sandwich signals two things: timing and development.

Most cheese needs to be refrigerated because of its large dairy content. Common cheeses are made from cow's milk, yet milk from other animals like goat, sheep, and buffalo are crowd-pleasers as well. But no matter what kind of cheese it is, if you leave cheese out at room temperature for too long, it will spoil. When it's refrigerated, however, and only taken out when it's ready to be served, the cheese becomes a wonderful part of the sandwich.

Just like knowing when to take the cheese out of the refrigerator for your sandwich, it is equally important in communication. The cheese is your timing and having the proper timing is important throughout an entire conversation. The more prepared you are via research and development of your opening, your segue, and your closing lines for your conversation or speech, the better your chances of being favorably received.

The type of conversation you need to have will determine the kind of cheese you will need for your sandwich. Take for example a conversation with a person or group to deliver a message about change or bad news. When it is something like this, the right timing is essential.

Some experts say that news of layoffs, salary freezes or closings should be made at the end of the day, and toward the end of the week so that the news doesn't negatively impact productivity.

As a leader, when these kinds of changes are happening, you need to be fully aware that most of your team will be adverse to it. Change is hard for most people and I believe that it is human nature to resist it. It's easy to become complacent and spoiled.

So when delivering this kind of news, consider using a mild, sweet cheese, like mozzarella or provolone. Keep in mind that when I say "mild" or "sweet," I am not saying that you should sugarcoat bad news. There is no way that you can always do that. But what you can do is be as honest, and as accurate as possible. You can communicate this news with a sense of empathy. This is also where you need to rely on the T.A.S.T.E. acronym, so you can fully access, test, and stabilize the environment before you discuss the dramatic change.

Now while it is important to add cheese to your sandwich, the cheese can either enhance or detract from your communication. If you use too much cheese, the person may be offended. The conversation could turn negative because the person may believe that you are either too lazy or thoughtless to research his issue to consider his point of view. And if you use too little cheese, the person may think that you don't care about them or the news that you're sharing.

Timing of the cheese and which cheese you should use is that you must get to the point, and move the conversation along with an enhanced cheese to make your listener feel good about himself and better about the situation. If you waste too much time, the cheese on your sandwich can spoil, and ruin all of your initial preparation. Don't let a great sandwich become bad.

Now sometimes due to things beyond your control, the sandwich *will* go bad. If it does, regroup and build it over again. It won't hurt to repeat key items, which helps bring your point home.

Cheese can be inserted into *any* layer of your sandwich. Therefore, depending on your subject, don't be afraid to add slices of cheese where you think the conversation may become confusing or difficult to swallow. Always consider the personality of the listener, especially if you are in a one-on-one situation and try to keep an open mind while moving the conversation to the point where you see quick closure. Your goal is to leave a sweet taste in the listener's mouth, at the right time.

One thing that is important to note is that listening has to be done by both parties. Not only are you speaking and communicating, but being a skillful communicator also means being a good listener. So listen as much as you speak, listen attentively, ask questions, and always give the person or the group you're speaking to an opportunity to speak and ask questions as well.

Another book that may help you to understand this concept is *Who Moved My Cheese?* by Dr. Spencer Johnson. In this book, cheese was used as a metaphor for change in an easy to comprehend parable to help readers see change in their lives from a creative perspective.

In his book, Dr. Johnson used four main characters: two mice, Sniff and Scurry, and two little people, Hem and Haw. All four characters live in a maze and spend their time roaming around in a constant pursuit of cheese. The uniqueness of each character is that they all have their own distinct personality like all of us, whether it be in our thought process, diligence or personal experiences.

In the story, Hem and Haw find the largest piece of cheese

imaginable and they decide there is no need to look for cheese ever again. Sniff and Scurry on the other hand, continue to explore their surroundings and stay in tune with their changing environment, because they soon realize that the cheese supply is dwindling down to nothing.

The little people, Hem and Haw, initially feared the life-altering change, yet Haw eventually followed Hem in search of new cheese. In the end, the book teaches a great lesson-that change is inevitable and we all will deal with it differently.

What did you do when your cheese was moved? Did you celebrate it? Did you remain stuck in the old cheese maze while new ones were being built all around you? The choice is yours. Changing your perspective of every situation will help you see the value in another point of view. Consider your team and evaluate the best ways to communicate change.

Sweet Peppers:

Timing is the key to effective communication. Equally important is your preparation for the conversation. If you know your team or audience's emotional quotient, ensure that you are speaking to them in the style, tone, and environment they are comfortable with. There is no use delivering an important message if no one is tuned in.

EAT UP!

Potential Customer
Always be honest and transparent; word of mouth will travel about your high integrity

🍴 Demonstrate your expertise early.

🍴 Do your homework and demonstrate a shared value in working together.

🍴 Be proactive and problem-solve before an issue arises.

Chapter 5
THE LETTUCE

Your Reasoning

"Come now, let us reason together," says the LORD

- Isa. 1:18 (ESV)

When God gave me this sandwich theme, the Scripture above immediately came to mind. However, instead of "let us" reason together, the words were clearly spelled l-e-t-t-u-c-e. My initial reaction was, *Wow this is deep!* God gave me a creative version of a homophone to express this sandwich preference. A homophone is a word with the same sound as another word, yet spelled differently with a different meaning. Words like "wood/would" and "one/won" for example. As you can see, my homophone has a twist, but for our purposes, we will use "lettuce reason together" for our sandwich.

Lettuce is an important ingredient to a sandwich because many varieties contain health benefits. Certainly Romaine has a better nutritional value than Iceberg. Romaine lettuce has a great deal of protein, calcium, iron, vitamins K, C, and A, as well as weight loss benefits. If lettuce is reasoning, why not look to fill-up your conversation with reason?

It would be great if in any conversation both parties understood that they are working together to mutually seek a favorable outcome. When Jesus said, let us come together, He was being optimistic about the communication. Likewise, we should go into discussions with a positive attitude despite the fact that we know there will be uncomfortable subjects discussed. A rule of thumb is to be optimistic, and use reasoning to complete your message.

Still, even with being optimistic, we will encounter difficult people at some point in our lives. Whether a friend, spouse, child, or a stranger, there is no doubt that unreasonable people are walking the planet every day. Who knows, maybe you are considered the unreasonable one. Regardless, if you know your conversation is going to be with a difficult person, then it's up to you to be prepared.

If you find yourself in this situation, first, open the discussion in a calm, whole wheat manner to invoke transparency so that from the very beginning both sides understand what the conversation is about. Second, quickly get to the meat, then add cheese to sweeten the message. If at this point you are making headway, add a few slices of lettuce to convince an unreasonable person to see your point of view.

Do your best to communicate your point and remain calm. The person may never get it, but feel confident that your role in delivering the message has been accomplished. Don't get frustrated over whether everyone will get you or not. They won't. Worrying about it, or trying to figure them out, is a pure waste of time. Your goal is to deliver the message clearly and concisely. You cannot always be responsible for the way the message is received. Yet the key is to always aim to add lettuce to your conversation to complement your sandwich.

Sweet Peppers:

Let's face it, homophones can be both confusing and funny. If you have a chance to share a lighter moment with your listener over a semantic error, play around with it and send them a nonsensical email message like, "Make sure you inform the **colonels** that there were **four** boxes of **kernels** of popcorn **for guests** that **guessed** which **kneaded** bread **needed** to be included with the **pairs** of **pears** for the **gorillas** that **rode** on the dangerous **road** with the **guerillas**." *I could go on and on...*

Chapter 6
THE TOMATO

Your Semantics

"The single biggest problem in communication is the illusion that it has taken place."

- George Bernard Shaw

Most of us think of a tomato as a vegetable, but it is actually a fruit. We all enjoy the diversity of a tomato either sliced on a sandwich, tossed in salad, as a sauce, or even as a juice. Not to mention the pounds of ketchup we eat each year. For our open-faced sandwich, adding a tomato to our communication serves as both a semantic cue and the option to deliver your message in a variety of ways.

Take this memorable tune from the 1937 classic, Shall We Dance with Fred Astaire and Ginger Rogers.

*"You like potato and I like potahto You like tomato and I like tomahto Potato, potahto, Tomato, tomahto.
Let's call the whole thing off..."*

- George Gershwin

This song is a "play" on the pronunciation of words based on class distinction. Our comprehension and level of understanding of words is based on our background and culture. That's why word choice in communication is critical-especially words that are spelled the same, but have different meanings, or words that sound the same, but are spelled differently.

> *Taste This: The scientific name for "tomato" is Lycopersicon lycopersicum which means "wolf peach."* EN 12 *What contrast! A tomato is a wild, carnivorous, sweet, tasty fruit! Deciding if and when to throw on a tomato gives you great leeway in your conversation.*

Homonym: Bear Scare

It was the beginning of winter and a recent snowfall had blanketed a small town in Oklahoma.

A husband walked into the kitchen. As he dusted the snow off his head, he said to his wife, "Honey, it's a bear out there!"

"Really? Thank God you're okay! I just read that the black bear population is increasing."

Startled, the husband shook his head, and walked into another room. Semantics involves the dual or cultural meaning of words. In the English language, nearly every word has a direct meaning and a connotative meaning. Miscommunication occurs when a person's connotative meaning for a word differs from yours.

In the bear example, the word "bear" is a homonym which means it has different meanings, but is spelled the same. Granted, I used the word "bear' in jest here, but in addition to the wild anmal, it also means to support, to be firm, to produce, to press or push against, amongst other meanings. This can be quite confusing for someone whose native language is not English.

Back to the bear example, the husband, as the communicator, should have chosen a more precise word to describe the cold - he should have chosen a word that would have had the same meaning to his wife. Something like: "Honey, it's a real blizzard out there!"

Hopefully, if you encounter a miscommunication like this with your spouse, you can follow him into the room, make a joke about your error, and give him a "bear" hug.

From a business perspective, though, this kind of example is neither cute nor funny. There are many business losses due to miscommunication between associates, and semantics is often the culprit. This "play" on words can lead to loss of productivity or missed deadlines.

The challenges with semantics can be overcome by using precise language that has the same context for you as it does for your listener. During a conversation, check in with him or her to ensure that both of you are on the same page throughout the discussion, and make sure that you clarify any misunderstandings on the spot.

For clarity in communication, be as specific as you can as the following example shows:

"Did you say you needed five dozen donuts by three-o'clock?"

"Yes, that is correct. I need five dozen donuts by three-o'clock today." "Got it! We can accommodate your order this afternoon."

"Thank you."

With this example, there will be no misunderstanding as to what was ordered, the time that the order is needed, and even the day when the order will be delivered. This clarity will avoid confusion and misunderstanding.

However even with clarification, verifying, and using precise language, miscommunication may still occur because each person's interpretation of your words are processed through their own cultural experiences or filters. Therefore, if your communication involves orders, processes, or timelines, or anything that has to be precise, it is best to get the communication in writing to avoid confusion.

A Few Crumbs...

The thing I like about tomatoes is that they are so diverse with thousands of varieties. In the past, tomatoes were considered poisonous due to a number of myths and misinformation. Again, unlike the other sandwich communication ingredients, the diversity of the tomato lends itself to careful consideration of your word choice so that you and your listener are on the same page. Don't lose the credibility of your message in the communication by using dual or multiple meaning words.

Chapter 7
THE MAYO

Your Transition

"We've become so focused on the tiny screen that we forget the big picture, the people right in front of us."

- Regina Brett

Mayonnaise is not just a flavor enhancer, but also a smooth spread that helps with the digestion of food. The same way that you spread mayonnaise over bread, think of mayo in the same vein with communication.

That is my philosophy about communication. A conversation often needs to be spread over and smoothed out so that the points of the discussion can be delivered and accepted. By doing this, you can ensure that the conversation will be processed in such a way that the information is well received.

When is mayo needed? Very often, this will be determined before your conversation even begins. After performing an assessment, you may decide the person will need a little more "spread" or time so that they can understand the concepts and digest the information a bit better.

However, there are some situations where you may

already be in the middle of the conversation before realizing that the discussion is not going according to plan. At that time, you can step back, spread on the mayo, and then proceed, knowing that the conversation will move forward more easily.

Just remember that everyone may need a little mayo here and there and there's nothing wrong with that. There's no need for a conversation to be rough, when with just a little bit of mayo, it can go down smooth.

Sweet Peppers:

Consider tasting these common "mayo" transition words:

"and" " also" "in addition" "for example" "furthermore" "instead" "likewise" "or" "so" "therefore"

EAT UP!

Manager to Employee

🍴 Put yourself in the employee's shoes when dealing with personal issue.

🍴 Show empathy and try to include yourself when speaking.

"Taste is the common sense of genius."

- *Victor Hugo*

Chapter 8
THE MUSTARD

Your Complexity

"When dealing with people, remember you are not dealing with creatures of logic, but creatures of emotion."

- Dale Carnegie

There are some topics that are just not as straightforward as others. You may have to discuss, for example, a technological process that became a problem as the result of an employee's error. Or there may be some other issue such as not approving a particular project or strategy where your conversation will have to be a complex one. These are not simple discussions and this is where you have to consider the mustard.

Taste This: *Before mustard was known as a condiment, it was used for medicinal purposes to relieve muscle aches and cure toothaches. Mustard clears sinuses and increases blood circulation. Use your mustard wisely to clear the air in difficult conversations or a complex subject matter.* EN 13

Mustard comes from tiny mustard seeds and is available in a variety of flavors and colors. They are grounded to satisfy taste buds ranging from sweet to spicy. You have to determine which type of mustard to use on your sandwich based on your listener:

Spicy - the person is a "know-it-all," and you must be bold, but respectful with your position, because you too are knowledgeable in the area

Yellow - the person has been moody or emotional in the past, and you are not sure who will show up, so proceed with caution.

Honey - the person is reasonable and kind, and you have had difficult conversations with him in the past, but you've always come to a mutual understanding.

Do a little research and have background on the person you will be speaking with. Again, choose your condiments wisely as they will help you achieve your desired communication outcome.

A Few Crumbs...

Mustard is more complex than the other optional sandwich ingredients. Since no two people are alike, technically, every communication whether one-on-one or to a group can ultimately be complex. There are so many factors that go into a discussion, which you need to be aware of to have a comfort level in reaching a positive outcome.

Chapter 9
THE SALT & PEPPER

Your Flavor & Your Disposition

"You are the salt of the earth, but if salt has lost its taste, how shall its saltiness be restored? It is no longer good for anything except to be thrown out and trampled under people's feet."

- Matthew 5:13

Salt has two purposes: to preserve food and to enhance the flavor of food. Too much salt in our daily diet can be deadly. However, despite the constant bad press about salt, the human body requires an adequate intake of salt to maintain good health. Salt has been a vital ingredient for centuries to preserve food from spoiling before there was any kind of refrigeration. When Jesus told His disciples that they were the salt of the Earth, He was telling them that they were now the preservatives of the world-preserving the world from inherent evil and sin.

> **Taste This:** *The word salary comes from the Latin word "salarium" and has the root "sal" or "salt." In ancient Rome, salt was an expensive, yet essential commodity that was paid to the Roman soldiers. EN 14 Just imagine the amount of money you could make if you knew how to throw your salt around!*

When we look to salt as a flavor enhancer, Christians are supposed to stand out to enhance the flavor of this world. So, when you are in a chaotic situation or conversation, as the salt, you should be in control with your positive attitude, tone, and body language. Where there is strife, you are the peacemaker. Your job is to take the high road by adding the right flavor to the conversation. If there is any type of hatred, you are to demonstrate the love of God. Don't be afraid to add the right amount of salt to your sandwich, which should be a sign to the listener that you are there to come to an agreement.

As I mentioned earlier, if you have a salty personality, or are known to engage in salty communications, your message will fall on deaf ears because your antics will ultimately lead to discord.

Likewise, pepper can do the same to your conversation. Pepper stimulates the taste buds and can definitely stimulate a conversation. When you think of pepper, you think of hot. However, pepper can also have health benefits such as improving digestion.

Too much pepper in your conversation, with a defensive or aggravated disposition, will detract from your message. Pepper can also be viewed as delivering bad news or taking a hard "No" stance that may not be popular with the majority. Keep in mind that you have to be "on," and let the other person know that you intend to be engaged in the conversation. This also means that you are cognizant of your tone, and facial expressions. Using the right amount of salt and pepper can turn a difficult conversation into an amicable one.

Chapter 10
TASTEFUL TIPS

#1 THE HEAT
Your Temperature

"Great leaders are almost always great simplifiers, who can cut through argument, debate and doubt, to offer a solution everybody can understand."

- Colin Powell

All sandwiches aren't meant to be heated, yet most open-faced sandwiches taste better when heated. What do you do when your conversation becomes heated? A gentle answer turns away wrath, but a harsh word stirs up anger [EN 15]. As the leader or initiator, it is up to you to begin the cooling down process. No one bites right into a hot sandwich. You have to let it cool off. How long you let it cool off depends on how the sandwich is heated.

We all look to the microwave as a quick fix, but it can be an unhealthy option. Microwave heating will leave your sandwich hard and inedible after a few minutes in the open. It can also easily burn your sandwich, which means that your sandwich will no longer be tasty.

Using a quick fix microwave discussion is just as ineffective.

This technique won't work because you may find yourself agreeing to an issue just to get the conversation over with. You may want to walk away because of the build up of tension in the room. If that happens, nothing will be resolved. Chances are, you will end up meeting with that irritable, disagreeable, person again anyway, over the same issue.

A traditional oven will heat the sandwich, but it may take longer as ovens need to be preheated first. Sometimes taking too long, trying to calm someone down, or figuring out how to offer another viewpoint during a heated discussion, may diminish your original message. You'll probably backtrack when you really did not want to, and by doing that the other person may believe that you have given in. More than likely, you opened the door for more questions and issues than you intended. Then, you will have to schedule another meeting to re-emphasize and make your points clear. Either way, a cooling off period will do everyone some good.

I believe the convection oven heating method for your sandwich is the best option. It offers a shorter cooking time, and thorough, air-circulated heat to cook your sandwich evenly. Convection ovens also work great to brown your sandwich, and "browning" during a conversation can serve to "warm each other down." You will still be required to take the lead in offering a cooling off moment. However, with each person having the opportunity to calm down and begin again on an even playing field, it is highly likely you will end your discussion with a satisfying resolution.

When you think about it, with so many personalities and challenges we face each day, amicable, smooth discussions are few and far between. What if you are finishing your sandwich, and the other party changes his mind about the discussion and adds something you never contemplated? Now, you become tense and the other person is agitated because of your reaction to his comment. Think fast. Your room temperature sandwich is now hot, and needs to be cooled down.

Peel back a few layers of your sandwich so that both of you can understand this sudden disconnect. First, reiterate the meat, which was the most important point of the conversation in the first place. If the meat is now your point of contention, write down the other party's issues and offer to reschedule the discussion so you have more time to consider your position. If the meat is not an issue, then you can move on to the other ingredients. You have a better chance of being on common ground if you and the other party differ on options, like semantics or flavor enhancers.

Sweet Peppers:

Oftentimes, you can deflect a person's anger by shifting their emotional outburst to something they can relate to or understand. Talk about yourself. Tell them you have been where they are, and there is no need going about the conversation in a heated manner; it will not be fruitful. Don't engage in the blame game or argue back. You can always agree with the person in theory.

#2 - THE CUT
Your Release

There is a time for everything,
and a season for every activity under the heavens...

- Ecclesiastes 3:1

Regardless of your communication techniques, some relationships have to be cut for the betterment of both parties. The sooner you realize that people come into our life for a reason, a season, or a lifetime, the better off you'll be. Like a sandwich, when you cut it in half, each side remains intact with identical ingredients on the other side. Both sides are balanced, and no one side has more than the other. Most people don't like to split their sandwich because it can get a little messy, but severing may be necessary. As you strive to be a whole wheat leader, your goal should be to nurture your staff, so that they move on and carry out the same qualities you represented to them, as they embark on new endeavors.

If there's one thing I've learned from being a leader all these years, it is that leading by example is one of the most fulfilling gifts you can give to your staff. I received a copy of a letter from a former staff member written in response to an editor's inquiry of leadership impact:

They say the apple doesn't fall too far from the tree. Sometimes your tree isn't your bloodline, but it is always your lifeline. I had the honor of being on a great leader's staff for eight years, and have received his spiritual counsel for 16 years and counting. The lessons I learned under his tutelage were invaluable, and have propelled my executive career in the nonprofit world. The vital lessons about succession planning, system implementation (those dreaded checklists!), and the iconic "don't let the method taint the message" approach to dealing with difficult colleagues, and clients have all been ingrained into me forever.

A few months after being hired at my current organization as a program director, my CEO was intrigued about where I gained my adeptness at dealing with staff conflict and handling multiple projects. There was one day in particular, where we had an unusually high amount of staff "concerns" and member grievances, all while

handling tight grant deadlines. I appeared unmoved by the enormity of the day and he asked me how I was able to cope and keep smiling through it all. I shared with him the concept of not letting the method taint the message, and who I learned it from. He said, "Remind me to thank that gentleman one day." Two months later, I was promoted to second in command, as the Chief Operating Officer. I am in my dream job, and I know that those
    lessons learned from years prior, have had a direct influence on my current success.
    My CEO crossed paths with my former leader one day, shook his hand, and remembered to thank him, as he acknowledged that he is currently benefitting from those prior teachings that I received. There are some relationships that no matter how they change in structure, they will always have a significant impact on your life. They are your lifeline, your tree. This apple hasn't fallen too far from hers.

Even though this employee left the company, she did so with invaluable experience, a positive attitude, and definitely on a high note. All of the seasonings in her sandwich represented growth. She took all of the good qualities from her communicative experiences that were necessary to help her succeed. It was my job to make sure that she had everything she needed to move forward in her next career opportunity.

Consequently, if you are not faced with an acrimonious separation, view it as a constructive one because everything was not meant to be together forever. Even if you have to fire a person, do everything within your power to make that person feel the relationship ended on good terms.

Chapter 11
EXTRA TOPPINGS

Nonverbal communication

"When the eyes say one thing, and the tongue another, a practiced man relies on the language of the first."

- Ralph Waldo Emerson

Keep in mind that a large percentage of communication is nonverbal. Not just body language, but gestures, appearance, posture, facial expressions, voice tone and even tattoos! All of these nonverbal details say a lot about a person. When we use gestures like waving, pointing or thumbs up or down, we probably don't realize that we are using them to communicate. Notwithstanding cultural differences, gestures are common communication vehicles when we are in a rush or are familiar with the other person.

A dead giveaway to a person's character is the clothes or hairstyle he or she chooses to wear when meeting you. If a person shows up for a job interview in workout gear, then his lack of professionalism may also come out when dealing with others. Finally, tone of voice, inflection, and pitch, are crucial nonverbal cues that could change the meaning of your statements.

Whether you are standing or sitting across from the person, try to ensure that you are using a positive voice tone, and that you are not speaking too fast or too slow. Stay away from mumbles, sighs and groans because the listener will quickly pick up that you don't want to be there-as if you have the *I'd rather be golfing* attitude. I also want to caution you to use the right words, and if you don't know the meaning of a word, don't use it! People will remember your poor word choice and lose (or not be able to hear) the rest of your message.

In my open-faced sandwich method, an easy word to remember is B.R.E.A.D. The BREAD acronym will be used in other tips as it contains key elements you should be aware of to engage your listener (s), or eventually end the relationship:

B = Body Language
R = Reiterate Understanding
E = Eye Contact
A = Ask Questions
D= Departure

EXTRA TOPPING BODY LANGUAGE

"The most important thing in communication is hearing what isn't said."

- Peter F. Drucker

A while back I had a meeting with a volunteer to inquire about a verbal altercation between her and another volunteer after Communion service. "Pastor, I barely spoke a word to her!"

"Okay, I wasn't there. So do you know why she was upset and crying this morning after leaving your post?"

"I have absolutely, positively, no idea."

Each time this woman spoke, not only did she wear a nervous smile, but she nodded her head in agreement. Studies have shown that conflicting body language such as this, is a sign of being untruthful. At that moment, I knew who was telling the truth. Her words said, "No," but her body language said, "Yes."

As the speaker, always remember that your body language can speak louder and clearer than anything you have to say. I knew from her nervous smile and the nodding of her head that she was being untruthful. I advised her that as a senior member, she needed to show concern for new members and bring them up to speed on any areas or functions they volunteered for.

A person's body language is a strong signal as to how they feel about your message and the level of respect she has for you as the speaker. If she is sitting upright and attentive, then she is interested in what you have to say. Slouching in her seat with her arms crossed is a sign of disinterest, and your message has fallen on deaf ears.

As a speaker or leader in a one-on-one setting, try to mirror the other person's body language. This levels the playing field and makes the listener comfortable with your approach. Make sure you are not too close or too far away from the person you are speaking with. If you are within a foot or two away, then that is too close, and the person may feel intimidated or uncomfortable that you are invading her personal "bubble" space. She will probably tune you out because she is distracted by the fact that you are literally "in her face." Yet, if you are more than ten feet away, then you are definitely too far and will come across as stand-offish. A good rule of thumb is to be about three to four feet away from your listener.

Keep in mind that the body language of men and women will be different. Men usually appear more confident and take up more space than women.

Another key body language tip includes watching out for your posture as the speaker. If you are in an open stance and your arms are at your sides, it sends a signal that you are approachable and looking forward to the conversation. Yet, if your arms are crossed and your shoulders hunched, that can send a negative message. Seeing that, the listener may feel you are unapproachable-that is, you could care less about the conversation taking place.

From another perspective, it can be difficult entering into communication with openness if you have a negative history with your listener. If you shut down based on past experiences in dealing with the issue or an individual, then you will miss the opportunity to hear new insight, or witness growth or change in the other person. Your job is to be totally open. This is the mantra of an open-faced communication sandwich; one slice of bread and your choice of meat and toppings in full view. No hidden agenda, bias, or distractions from effectively discussing your point and coming to agreement.

I chuckle about it now, but I recall being in a meeting where two volunteers were about to come to blows over an issue. Each of the men were adamant about their point and a shouting match ensued to the extent that they had to be separated. After I calmed the men down, I immediately saw that one of the men was convicted and genuinely embarrassed by his actions, while the other was still fuming. I gave them both time to reflect and offered them something to drink.

After some time had passed, we broached the subject again, and the "fuming" guy was still on fire. He totally shut down to what his colleague had to say-even to the point where when his colleague agreed with him on several positions, he remained closed off and angry. He wasn't even aware of their mutual agreement.

Having a closed mind will cause you to miss out on key interactions that may be necessary for you to move your message forward and grow in the process. More importantly, if you remain closed-minded, you will miss the satisfying taste and fullness of coming to an agreement and having your point understood.

EXTRA TOPPING
REITERATE UNDERSTANDING

"Any idea, plan, or purpose may be placed in the mind through repetition of thought."

- Napoleon Hill

I really enjoy the Geico commercials every few months with different actors spreading the exact same message. Geico has embarked on one of the most clever advertising campaigns in recent memory, by poking fun at their own repetition of the same message: "Did you know Geico can save you 15 percent on car insurance? Everybody knows that!" Forget about the cavemen, office workers, and guitar strumming singers; even my grandchildren know the words to these commercials! That's because of repetition. The commercial is played over and over.

One of the main reasons for writing this book stemmed from my frustration with disconnects in staff communications after critical meetings. I quickly discovered that newer staff members had a vague idea of plans being discussed, while the legacy members often tuned out because they assumed they heard it all before. It took me a while to realize that repetition was the key.

At first, I didn't want to sound like a broken record. Then it hit me. Since we were children, we learned by repetition. As we grew older, we continued to learn by repetition because repetition increases the likelihood of our understanding. In my production challenges, in order to ensure that I avoided major disconnects, twice a month, I provided a duplicate "refresher" talk to team leaders. Just like Geico, I repeated my message to ensure optimum understanding.

In addition, our church performs several productions every year. Each season we utilize staff, legacy volunteers, and we recruit new volunteers. During production meetings, I provided input on how certain programs should run because every year, I wanted to give the audience a twist or a little more than the previous year.

Oftentimes in these meetings, I left out many of the details because I was confident that my legacy team knew exactly what I meant. I recall on several occasions, I said to them, "Make it happen!" After the meeting, the new regime left the table with the program concept, minus the details. Both the new and old regime clashed. I chuckle at it now because the new regime was willing to "make it happen" at all costs, when the old team knew I meant within budget, and in compliance with church guidelines.

What did I learn from this experience? I learned that I needed to have a clear and cohesive message so that the new and old team heard the same thing. My communication disconnect came from my assumption that the new people got what they needed from the legacy team. Today, I have a system in place to assimilate new team members into the process. This system has created a strong fabric for weaving in the old and new. After the initial training, I schedule a meeting to reiterate the program processes no matter how repetitive it sounds. I explain every detail, to ensure everyone is on the same page.

Sweet Peppers:

It's a good idea to repeat a message if you believe it is misunderstood. However, don't over explain and drag your new explanation out longer than the first. Consider using graphics to explain your message as well, because listeners who tune out of long messages may be drawn to a graphic that explains key points.

EXTRA TOPPING
EYE CONTACT

"The eyes are the window to your soul."

- *William Shakespeare*

The worst thing you can do in a one-on-one conversation is to never look your listener in the eye. This sends a glaring red flag to the other person that you are hiding something. Making eye contact is an important part of your body language that will help communicate the meat of your message. Your eyes are the focal point of your body. People naturally look at your eyes and focus on the "T" zone of your face.

Eye contact sends several messages simultaneously: 1) it tells the person that you respect her and view her as important, and ii) it builds trust and a connection. As soon as you open your mouth and begin to make eye contact, studies have shown that you will be perceived as honest, reliable, and sincere. Therefore, engage your listener quickly and make eye contact to begin your communication. The results are in your favor because the listener has already deemed you trustworthy.

EAT UP!

Relationships

Ψ Don't assume you know that the other person is thinking based on prior dealings-ask him.

Ψ Be cognizant of your body language, eye contact, and hand gestures.

EXTRA TOPPING
ASK QUESTIONS

"We run this company on questions, not answers."

- Eric Schmidt

We've all heard that there is no such thing as a bad question. Simply put, asking questions helps you find answers. It is also the most effective way of learning. The moment we begin to speak, our learning evolves by asking questions. As parents, we have answered at least a million "Why" questions from our toddlers. As adults, asking questions tells the speaker that you are fully engaged in the moment, which can lead to a more positive outcome of the meeting.

Remember those "know-it-all" enriched leaders who never asked their employees questions? You know, the ones whose answer is always right? Give them two thumbs down. Never get rid of an employee who asks a lot of questions because inquisitive minds can lead to your organization's breakthroughs. Take time to ask questions, to get a deeper understanding of daily business challenges.

Consider the leadership style of Mark Zuckerberg, Facebook's CEO. He interacts with his employees every Friday by updating everyone on the company's plans, and then holds a Q&A afterward. Leaders who think that they "know-it-all" will never reach higher levels of succcss.

EXTRA TOPPING DEPARTURE

"The only certain freedom's in departure."

- Robert Frost

The saying "all good things must come to an end" is true.

However, bad things should end in a timely manner as well. In all of our relationships, there may come a time when a parting of the ways is not only necessary, but inevitable. Through the years, I've learned that a parting doesn't have to be negative; both parties can benefit from an amicable departure, especially employees who were under whole-wheat leaders.

Sweet Peppers:

To maintain healthy relationships, you should evaluate your friendships, and consider your interactions with colleagues. It's okay to sever ties with those who bring you down, are constant pessimists, or judgmental. If this person is your leader, find ways to maintain your personal distance without being disrespectful or insubordinate.

Chapter 12
THE WRAP UP

Your satisfaction

It is finished! How did you get there? You started with your slice of whole wheat bread with an open approach to the conversation. You smoothed on mayo. You added the meat to ensure you made your point and it was understood-no semantic word-play. Depending on the subject matter of the conversation, you added cheese to ensure it was the right time to enhance your point and sweeten the deal. Maybe you added yellow mustard on top of the cheese to determine the person's mood. Then, you added your lettuce to demonstrate your willingness to reason with the other party. It's delicious and tasty, and more important, effective.

As you have seen, there are benefits to open communication. First, the listener feels empowered because he sees this as an opportunity to share his ideas. Once he believes his input for the current challenge is being heard, he is likely to be more creative and proactive in finding a solution. Second, as the leader, the more you share the company's vision and key insight that is not just reserved for the high level employees, the more buy- in you will have from everyone within the organization as a whole.

The table is set for you to commit time to practicing being open and aware of your verbal and nonverbal actions. If you do it right, you will notice how your team or anyone else you are communicating with walks away with a positive outcome. It's a good idea to wrap up by reiterating the meat, and then closing out the conversation with positive reinforcement and accolades.

Remember, if you are engaging with a sweet personality, you won't need as much mayo. A sour personality may need extra mayo and more cheese. Likewise, a salty character will probably need more meat upfront, so make your point quickly, and end the conversation. If you desire to add tomatoes, do so to ensure that both you and your listener are on the same page with your word choices. Be mindful that there may be cultural or other life experiences where common words to you may mean something different to others.

Finally, adding lettuce is the reasoning aspect of your conversation. Therefore, you may want to leave off the lettuce in your discussion with a bitter person since reasoning is probably not in their frame of reference. You will be very frustrated trying to convince this type of person to see your point of view. Instead, stick to your message with an appropriate tone, and try to finish on a positive note. It's okay if a bitter person doesn't "get it" right away. Over a period of time, she may come to understand when her circumstances and perspective changes.

Maintain your engaging and open personality with flavor throughout the discussion. When prepared right, your sandwich will be tasty to your palette and the person or group that you engage in conversation. Make sure that every ingredient you choose serves its communicative purpose.

Always keep in mind that communication does not mean that you always have to agree. The key ingredient here is how do you get past disagreement to make it work so that both parties feel satisfied. As on the day of Pentecost, everyone was with one accord even though they all still spoke different languages afterwards. Your sandwich is made up of various components, fitly joined together to help nurture the body; it is food for the soul. Building your effective communication sandwich requires a mutual effort to work with everyone as a team. so that others feel you have their best interest at heart to achieve your desired outcome.

Ensure that everyone on your team is using their gifts and talents, and collaborating to be successful. Always remember that a tasteful outcome in your daily communication is on the tip of your tongue, waiting to make a positive difference in someone's life. Go ahead, satisfy your appetite, one sandwich-worthy ingredient at a time!

OPEN-FACED SANDWICH MAKEOVER

Now that you've finished your Open-Faced Sandwich, take time to jot down situations where you can make actionable changes to becoming a more effective communicator.

THE TASTE : YOUR PALATE

1. What are some things you can do or have done in the past, to test the environment?

_____

_____

_____

_____

2. Can you recall tasteful adjectives others have used to describe you? Sweet, Sour, Salty, Bitter? What were the circumstances? What can you do to change any negative descriptions?

_____

_____

_____

_____

THE BREAD: YOUR PERSONALITY

3. Which type of bread leader did you identify with?
   Enriched, Whole Wheat, Multigrain, Flatbread, Rye,
   Hoagie? Why? Are you a combination of more than one?

_____

_____

_____

_____

4. Are there characteristics in your leadership style that
   you need to change? Think about your most recent
   conversation with a team member. Was it effective? Were
   you satisfied or frustrated with the outcome? What could
   you have said differently?

_____

_____

_____

_____

5. How has your personality helped or hindered your growth
   as leader? As a spouse? As a parent?

_____

_____

_____

_____

6. What can you do to encourage others to communicate like a whole wheat leader? How are you going to lead by example?

_____

_____

_____

_____

THE MEAT: YOUR POINT

7. What techniques did you use in the past to get to the point? How can the open-faced sandwich method help you improve to make your point clear?

_____

_____

_____

_____

THE CHEESE: YOUR TIMING & DEVELOPMENT

8. What is your track record for delivering bad news? Was your timing appropriate? How did your team or someone close to you react?

_____

_____

_____

_____

9. How much preparation did you put into your last discussion or group talk? What else could you have done to ensure your communication was well received?

_____

_____

_____

_____

THE MUSTARD: YOUR COMPLEXITY

10. If you have an upcoming conversation that is sensitive or difficult, write down a few opening lines to put your listener at ease.

_____

_____

_____

_____

THE TOMATO: YOUR FLAVOR

11. Semantics, experiences and cultural differences can lead to communication breakdowns. What happened during your last disconnect with your team or family member? How will you handle communication with this person going forward?

_____

_____

_____

_____

THE SALT & PEPPER: YOUR FLAVOR & DISPOSITION

12. Knowing when to add the right flavor to your communication is an important ingredient in your layering. What have you done recently to demonstrate your salt value? Also, consider using pepper and the appropriate mustard (spicy, yellow, or honey) for that same encounter.

_____

_____

_____

EXTRA TOPPINGS: THE HEAT, THE CUT

13. Thinking back on your last heated one-on-one discussion, how long did it take to cool down? Did you invoke a cooling off period and circle back to discuss? What was the outcome?

_____

_____

_____

14. List a few heated discussions that you had with a colleague or family member. Revisit that interaction and apply the convection oven type of reasoning to bring full closure. Meet with the person and put it to rest.

_____

_____

15. Whether you are releasing an employee or someone in your personal life, some cuts are necessary to grow. Consider some releases that you have made as well as some you need to make. What did you learn about yourself and the person you released? What will you do this time around to ensure that this upcoming release will be amicable?

_____

_____

_____

_____

16. What will you do if you realize you cut someone in haste? Do you have the humility to go back and try to mend? What if you left your employer and now want to go back? How can you apply the open-faced sandwich method to rebuild the relationship?

_____

_____

_____

_____

A Few Crumbs...

Now that you've gone through this open-faced sandwich exercise I hope you have come away with a greater understanding of your communication method and style, as well as what you need to portray to your listener. Don't think you can master this technique in one or two conversations. The more cognizant you are of your communications in applying this method, the better you will become over time. I guarantee you will feel less stressed.

ENDNOTES

1: Matthew 18:20

2: Acts 2:20

3: Isaiah 1:18

4: http://www.brainfacts.org/sensing-thinking-behaving/senses-and-perception/articles/2011/a-matter-of-taste/

5: Psalm 34:8

6: http://www.damascusbakery.com/2014/05/15/knew-bread-interesting-top-10-bread-facts-probably-didnt-know/

7: Acts 9:1-22

8: John 6:35

9: Philippians 2:5

0: John 13:27

11: http://www.statisticbrain.com/attention-span-statistics/

12: http://www.hgtvgardens.com/tomatoes/fun-facts-about-tomatoes

13: http://www.the-mustard-factory.com/mustard-facts

14: http://www.mortonsalt.com/salt-facts/fun-facts

15: Proverbs 15:1

A Few Crumbs...

I'd love to hear from you on how the open-faced sandwich method worked for you. Reach out to me by logging on to the website at theopenfacedsandwich.com to drop me a bite!

E. Earl Jenkins

E. Earl Jenkins is the founding pastor of True Servant Worship and Praise Church in Hamilton, New Jersey and True Servant Central, in Eatontown, New Jersey. He earned his Bachelor of Theology degree from the Eastern Bible College and received his Masters degree in Theology from Freedom Bible College and Seminary.

As President and CEO of EEJ Enterprises, a subsidiary of The Jenkins Group Inc., Mr. Jenkins oversees a variety of businesses that span an array of needs including clinical health, green-based cleaning supplies and services, as well as male mentoring programs and family entertainment. He is also the author of *Don't Hate Your Enemies Just Step on Them: The Art of Loving People.*

FOR MORE INFORMATION OR FOR BOOKINGS

LOG ON TO

www.theopenfacedsandwich.com

Made in the USA
Middletown, DE
27 April 2016